Huck Scarry

On Wheels

First published 1980 in the United States of America
by Philomel Books, The Putnam Publishing Group,
200 Madison Avenue, New York, NY 10016.
Text and illustrations copyright © 1980 by Huck Scarry.

PHILOMEL BOOKS

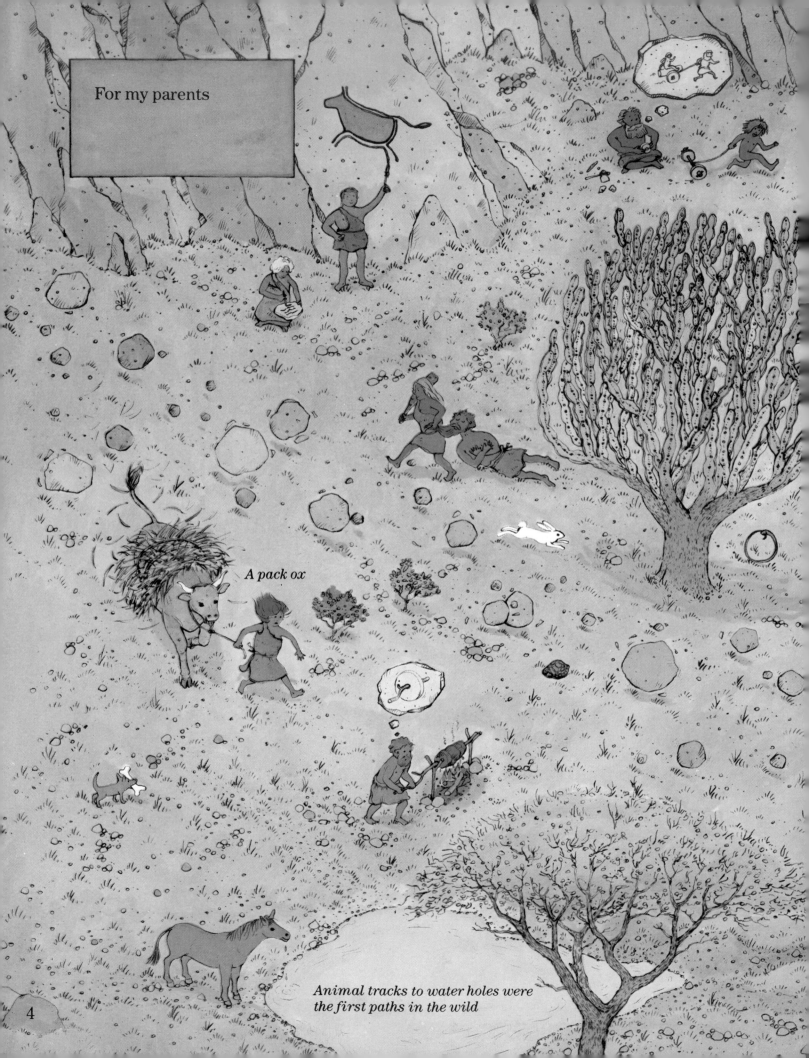

For my parents

A pack ox

Animal tracks to water holes were
the first paths in the wild

4

Long, long ago, long before anyone you know was born, there were no wheels anywhere. There were no carts, no bicycles, no roller skates, not even a wheelbarrow in the whole world! Everyone had to walk.

To move heavy loads, people placed them on the backs of animals. An animal like the ox, for example, could also be trained to pull a wooden sled. In this way it could carry much more.

Nobody knows who first had the idea to put rollers or wheels under a sled, but it certainly made pulling easier!

Let's join Peter Pebble as he travels through thousands of years and the pages of this book to discover more about wheels.

Look out for those rolling boulders, Peter, and for cavemen getting wheel ideas!

A rough ride on a log sled

The earliest tools could not cut a solid wheel from a tree trunk

A primitive log litter

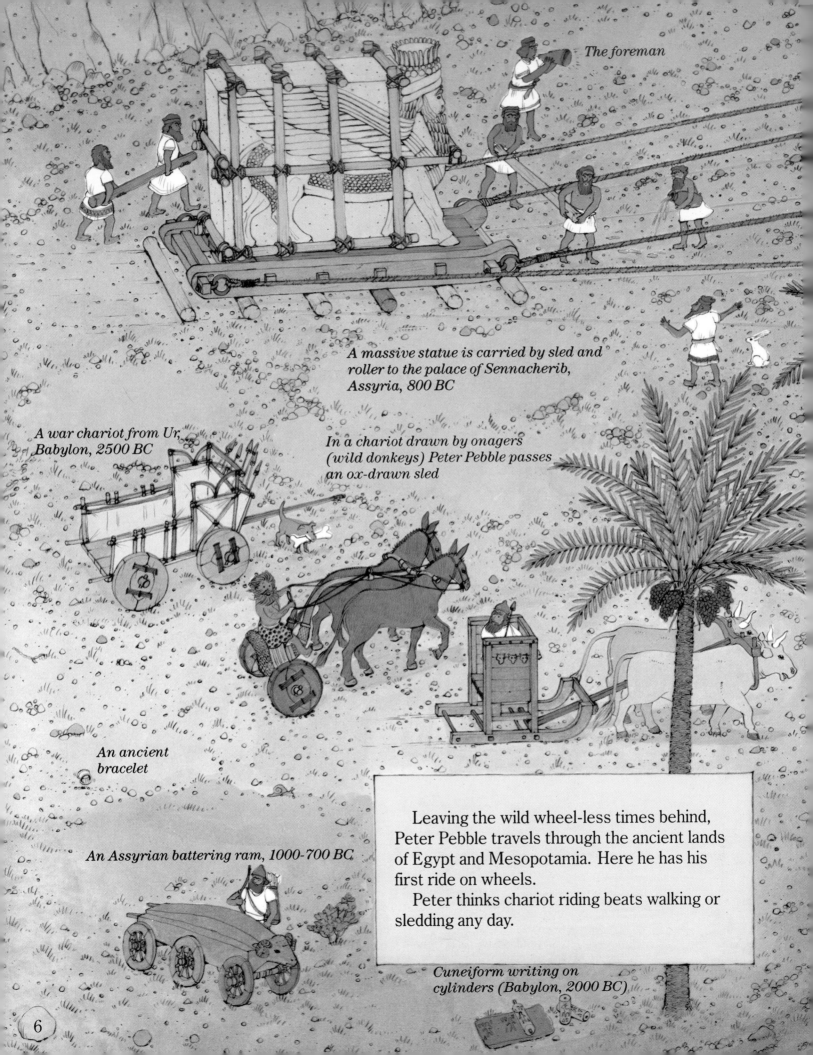

The foreman

A massive statue is carried by sled and roller to the palace of Sennacherib, Assyria, 800 BC

A war chariot from Ur, Babylon, 2500 BC

In a chariot drawn by onagers (wild donkeys) Peter Pebble passes an ox-drawn sled

An ancient bracelet

An Assyrian battering ram, 1000-700 BC

Leaving the wild wheel-less times behind, Peter Pebble travels through the ancient lands of Egypt and Mesopotamia. Here he has his first ride on wheels.

Peter thinks chariot riding beats walking or sledding any day.

Cuneiform writing on cylinders (Babylon, 2000 BC)

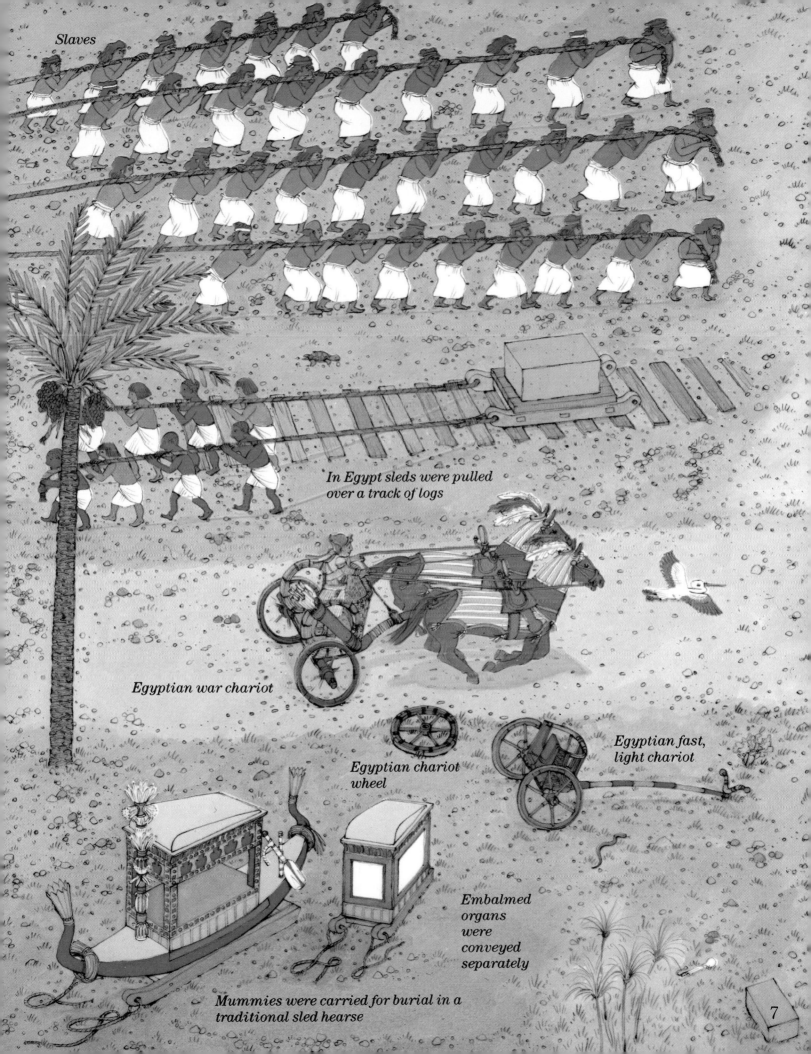

Slaves

In Egypt sleds were pulled over a track of logs

Egyptian war chariot

Egyptian chariot wheel

Egyptian fast, light chariot

Mummies were carried for burial in a traditional sled hearse

Embalmed organs were conveyed separately

7

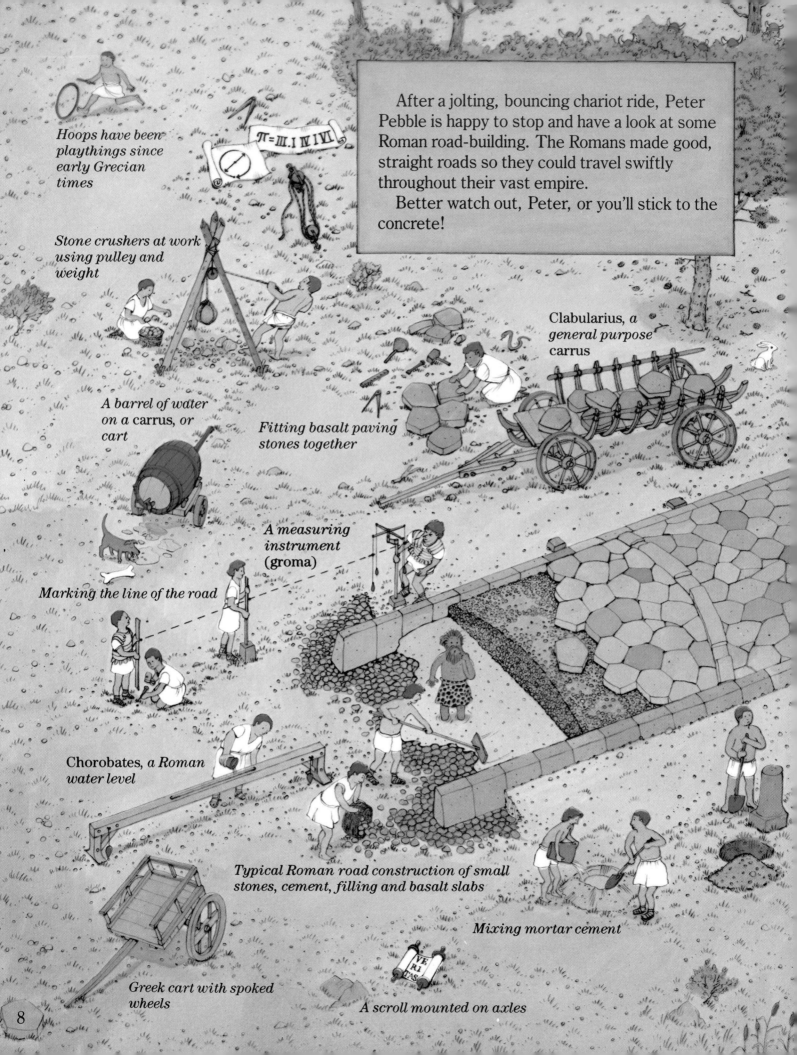

Hoops have been playthings since early Grecian times

π=Ⅲ.Ⅰ Ⅳ Ⅵ

Stone crushers at work using pulley and weight

After a jolting, bouncing chariot ride, Peter Pebble is happy to stop and have a look at some Roman road-building. The Romans made good, straight roads so they could travel swiftly throughout their vast empire.

Better watch out, Peter, or you'll stick to the concrete!

Clabularius, *a general purpose* carrus

A barrel of water on a carrus, or cart

Fitting basalt paving stones together

A measuring instrument (groma)

Marking the line of the road

Chorobates, *a Roman water level*

Typical Roman road construction of small stones, cement, filling and basalt slabs

Mixing mortar cement

Greek cart with spoked wheels

A scroll mounted on axles

Roman dart-thrower, carroballista

A *two-seater* carpentum

Letica, a Roman litter

Roman post-chaise (birotum)

Roman litter for women

Basterna, a Roman mule-drawn litter

A Roman hiker

Roman stone and wood bridge

An abacus

9

Flemish carriage wagon of 1347

An abandoned Roman carruca (wheeled throne)

Swiss wooden statue of Christ (c. 1200) for Palm Sunday procession

Wheelbarrow

Building a stone bridge using wooden scaffolding

Viking wagon

Onager, a Roman mobile catapult with a kick like a wild donkey

Celtic wagon from Denmark (100 BC)

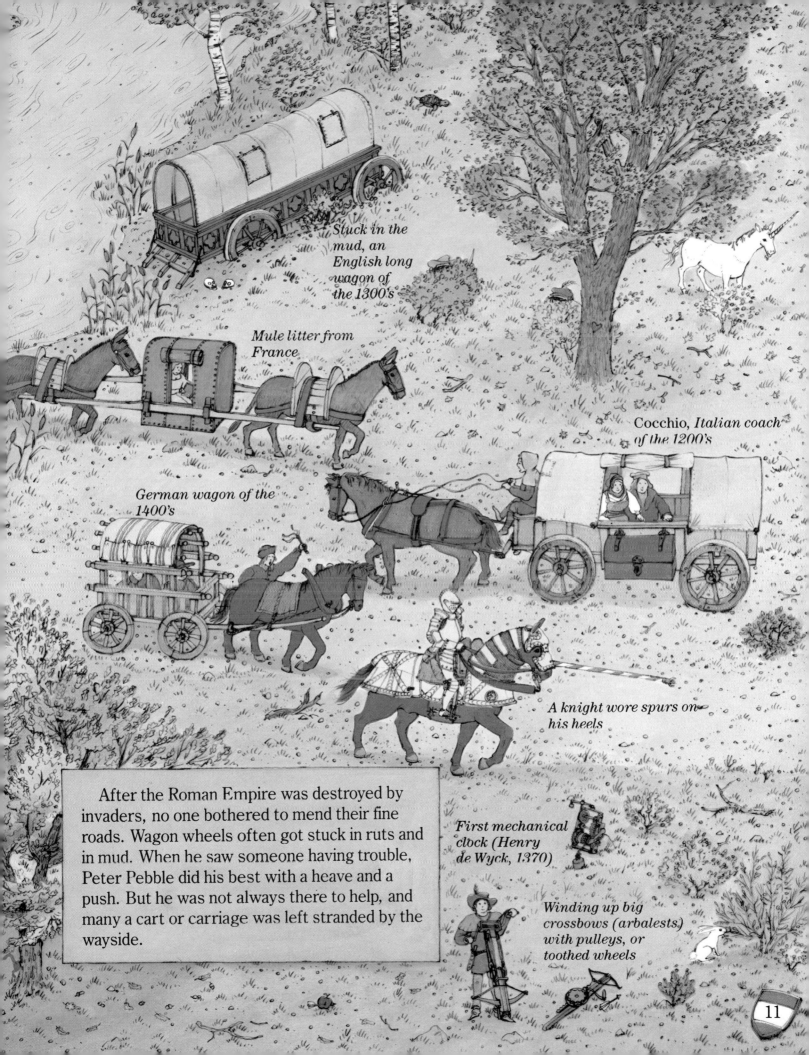

Stuck in the mud, an English long wagon of the 1300's

Mule litter from France

Cocchio, Italian coach of the 1200's

German wagon of the 1400's

A knight wore spurs on his heels

After the Roman Empire was destroyed by invaders, no one bothered to mend their fine roads. Wagon wheels often got stuck in ruts and in mud. When he saw someone having trouble, Peter Pebble did his best with a heave and a push. But he was not always there to help, and many a cart or carriage was left stranded by the wayside.

First mechanical clock (Henry de Wyck, 1370)

Winding up big crossbows (arbalests) with pulleys, or toothed wheels

Two English coaches of
the early 1600's

A stable for
horses

12

In 1543, Nicolaus Copernicus wrote about the solar system, or how the planets revolve around the sun

An English plow of the 1600's

Sedan chair (1655)

Duncombe sedan chair (1634)

A hackney coach (about 1630)

Inns provided warm meals and cozy beds for weary travelers. Horses could also be rented at the inn's stables. Peter Pebble has decided to hire one. He doesn't want to be in a carriage that is stuck in the mud. He may not know where he's going, but he knows where he's been!

One of the coaches of Queen Elizabeth of England (1500's)

An early globe of the earth (1492)

13

Simon Stevinus's sail wagon (1600)

Ship's wheel

Clinging on tightly, Peter Pebble is too busy at first to notice all the wheels around him. There are wheels that roll on the ground, and wheels that spin in the wind!

Two experimental French wind wagons (1714)

Surveyors

A graphometer (1597) measures angles

A weary wayfaring chandler

French coach (mid 1600's)

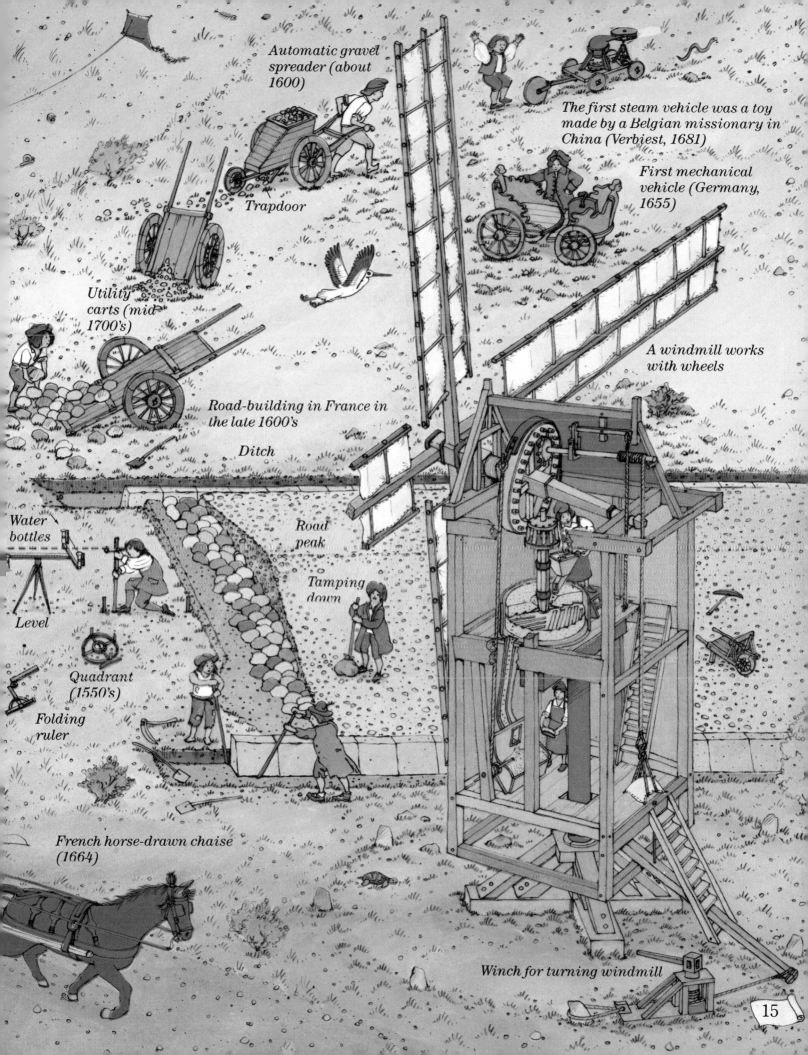

Automatic gravel spreader (about 1600)

Trapdoor

The first steam vehicle was a toy made by a Belgian missionary in China (Verbiest, 1681)

First mechanical vehicle (Germany, 1655)

Utility carts (mid 1700's)

A windmill works with wheels

Road-building in France in the late 1600's

Ditch

Water bottles

Road peak

Tamping down

Level

Quadrant (1550's)

Folding ruler

French horse-drawn chaise (1664)

Winch for turning windmill

15

The wheelwright's shop

Conestoga wagon (1750)

Making wheels at the wheelwright's

Off to the blacksmith for an iron rim

Horse's feed trough

A journeyman

Running gear of a Conestoga wagon

Sedan chair

Measuring wheel (traveler)

Hammering a hot metal rim onto a wooden wheel

Tongs for holding hot metal rim

Wheel and rim cooling in water

In a colonial American village, Peter Pebble sees how wheels were once made. Bang! Bang! Bang! He helps knock a hot metal rim onto a wooden wheel.

On the other side of the blacksmith's shop, his horse waits patiently on three legs. It is having a new shoe fitted.

The harness-maker

Colonial plow

American chaise of the late 1700's

American hickory shay (1755)

Shoeing Peter Pebble's horse

Pitching horseshoes

A pump

The blacksmith's shop

17

A plow of the mid 1700's

French public coach of the 1700's (carabas)

Sedan chair

French post-chaise (1700's)

French stagecoach of the mid 1700's

Count de Sivrac's hobbyhorse (1791)

French vinaigrette, suspended on piston springs

Dump-cart

Tamping tool

18

A gray funnel of smoke hisses into the air. Peter Pebble's horse rears up in fear, and tosses his rider backwards to the ground.

The world's first steam-powered wagon has just given Peter's horse the fright of its life!

English quarry wagon on rails, of the 1700's

Nicolas Cugnot's steam wagon (1770)

A berlin of the mid 1700's

French road of the 1700's made of large stones, gravel and pebbles

Berlin coupé

Milestones and surveyor's instruments

19

Richard Trevithick with two of his steam locomotives (1801-04)

Trevithick's steam road-engine (1803)

Lord Brougham's brougham (1837)

W. H. James's steam coach (about 1830)

The first railway passenger coach was built in 1825 by George Stephenson for the Stockton and Darlington Railway

Fish-bellied rails

20

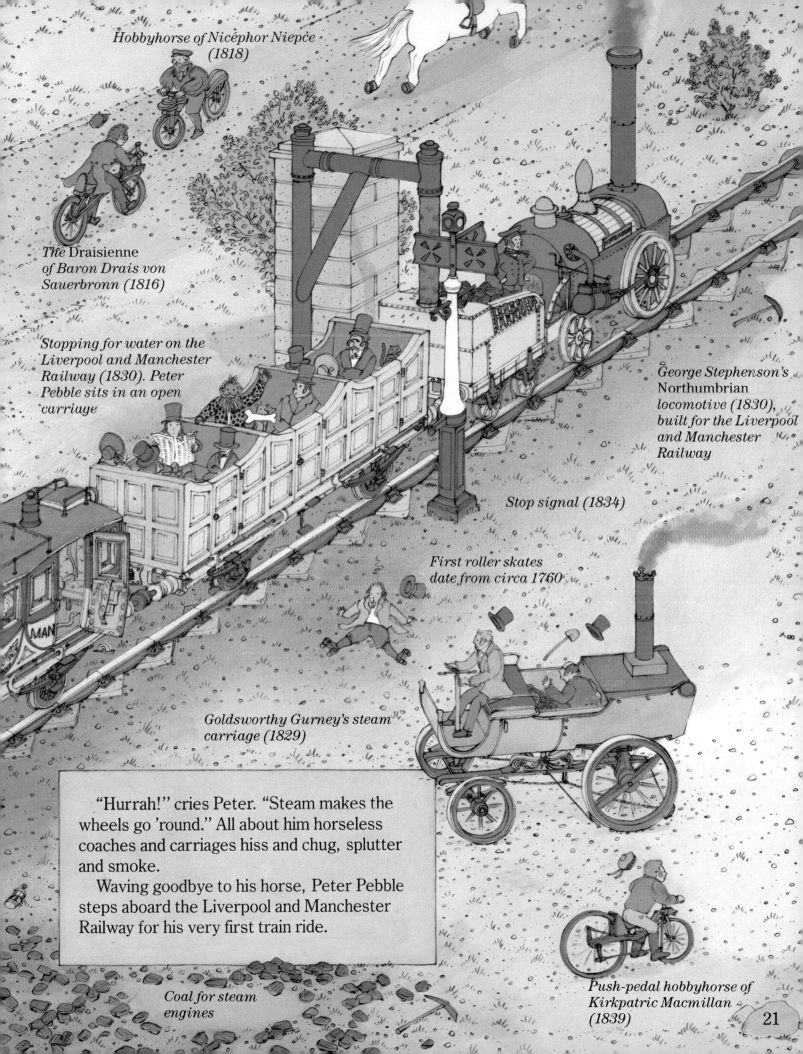

Hobbyhorse of Nicéphor Niepce
(1818)

The Draisienne
of Baron Drais von
Sauerbronn (1816)

Stopping for water on the
Liverpool and Manchester
Railway (1830). Peter
Pebble sits in an open
carriage

George Stephenson's
Northumbrian
locomotive (1830),
built for the Liverpool
and Manchester
Railway

Stop signal (1834)

First roller skates
date from circa 1760

Goldsworthy Gurney's steam
carriage (1829)

"Hurrah!" cries Peter. "Steam makes the
wheels go 'round." All about him horseless
coaches and carriages hiss and chug, splutter
and smoke.

Waving goodbye to his horse, Peter Pebble
steps aboard the Liverpool and Manchester
Railway for his very first train ride.

Coal for steam
engines

Push-pedal hobbyhorse of
Kirkpatric Macmillan
(1839)

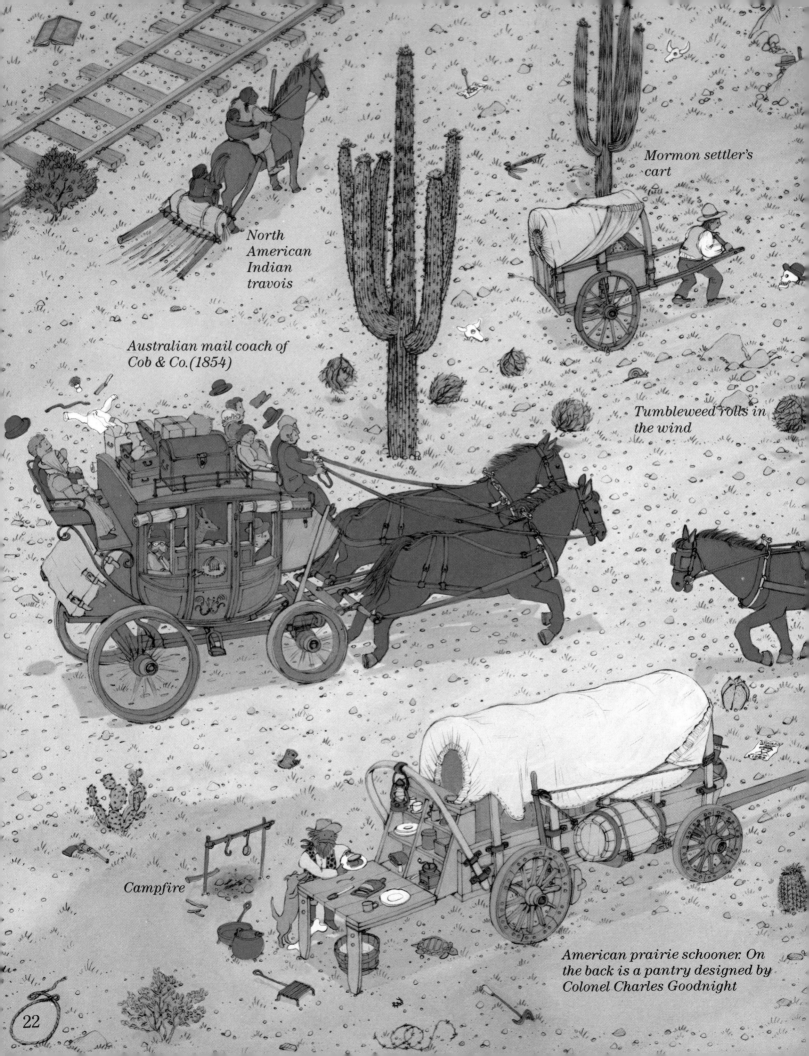

North American Indian travois

Mormon settler's cart

Australian mail coach of Cob & Co. (1854)

Tumbleweed rolls in the wind

Campfire

American prairie schooner. On the back is a pantry designed by Colonel Charles Goodnight

Boot spur

For travel over difficult trails the mud wagon stage was used

The Concord coach took its name from where it was built—Concord, New Hampshire (1870)

WELLS FARGO & CO.

U.S. MAIL

REWARD $1000

An American prospector's wagon

Arriving in the dusty Far West, Peter Pebble is happy to stop for a bite to eat.
"All this traveling makes me hungry!" he says, as he helps himself at the chuck wagon.
Watch out for bandits, Peter!

Wood and rawhide Red River cart built by settlers in Far West

Sharpening a knife on a grinding wheel

Some of the wheels found in the home

For comfortable travel in the 1800's the French built a sleeping carriage called a dormeuse

French steam bus by Lotz (1866)

The first pedal bicycle, France (1861)

A stone-boat

In 1863 Etienne Lenoir, a Belgian, designed a gasoline-powered car. It was never built

Windlass

A double-ended plow being hauled back and forth by steam tractor power

24

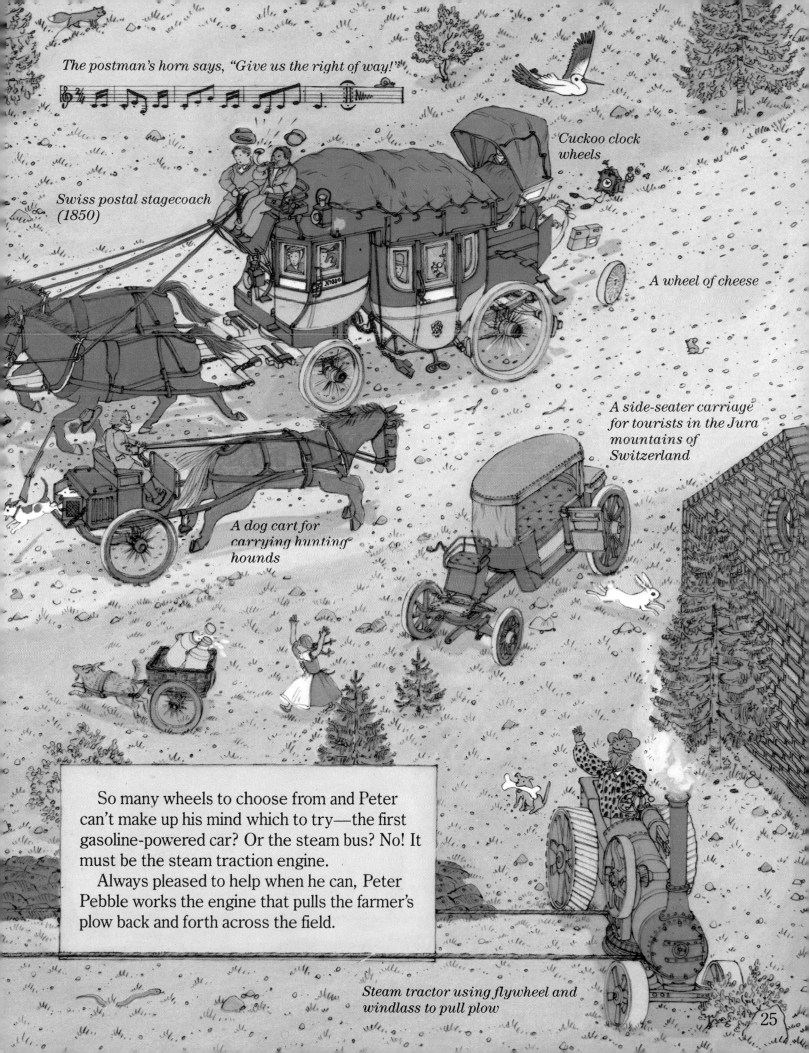

The postman's horn says, "Give us the right of way!"

Swiss postal stagecoach (1850)

Cuckoo clock wheels

A wheel of cheese

A side-seater carriage for tourists in the Jura mountains of Switzerland

A dog cart for carrying hunting hounds

So many wheels to choose from and Peter can't make up his mind which to try—the first gasoline-powered car? Or the steam bus? No! It must be the steam traction engine.

Always pleased to help when he can, Peter Pebble works the engine that pulls the farmer's plow back and forth across the field.

Steam tractor using flywheel and windlass to pull plow

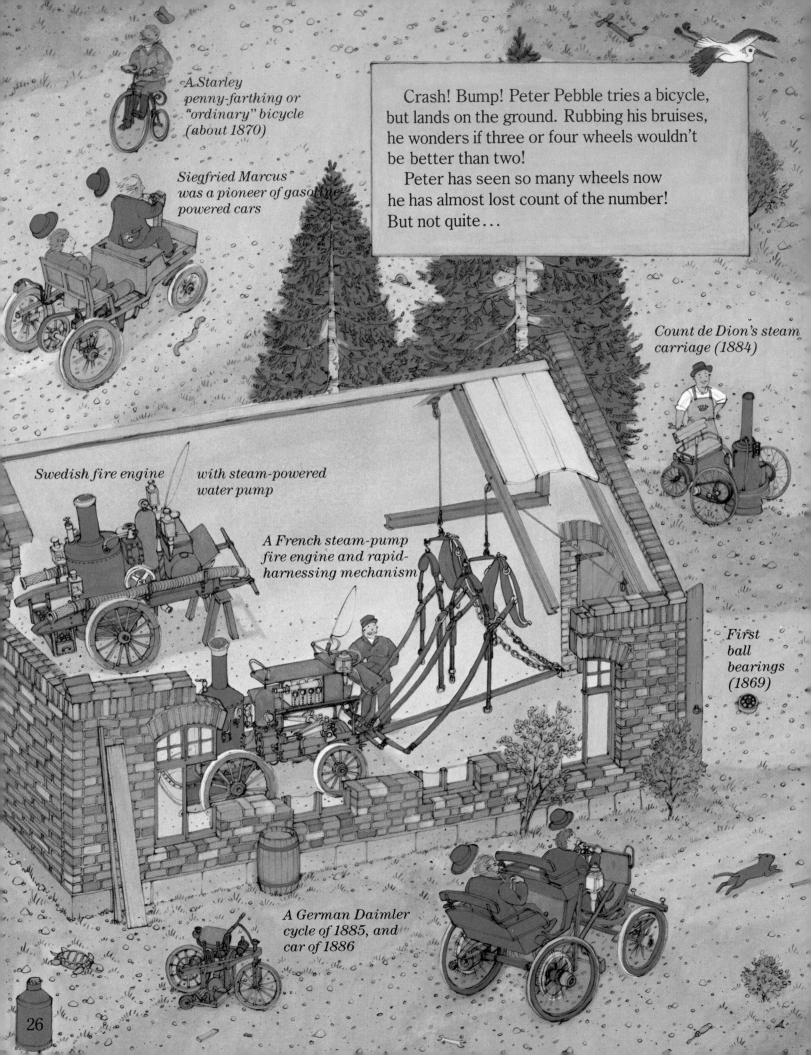

A Starley penny-farthing or "ordinary" bicycle (about 1870)

Siegfried Marcus was a pioneer of gasoline-powered cars

Crash! Bump! Peter Pebble tries a bicycle, but lands on the ground. Rubbing his bruises, he wonders if three or four wheels wouldn't be better than two!

Peter has seen so many wheels now he has almost lost count of the number! But not quite...

Count de Dion's steam carriage (1884)

Swedish fire engine with steam-powered water pump

A French steam-pump fire engine and rapid-harnessing mechanism

First ball bearings (1869)

A German Daimler cycle of 1885, and car of 1886

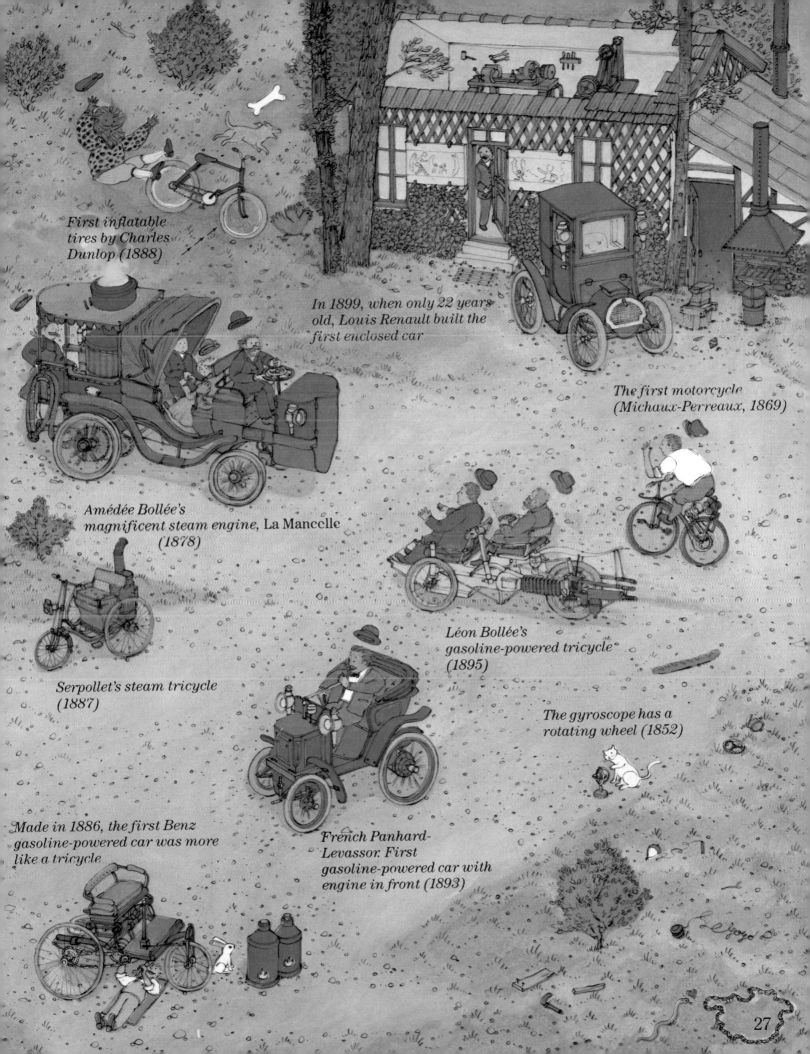

First inflatable tires by Charles Dunlop (1888)

In 1899, when only 22 years old, Louis Renault built the first enclosed car

The first motorcycle (Michaux-Perreaux, 1869)

Amédée Bollée's magnificent steam engine, La Mancelle (1878)

Léon Bollée's gasoline-powered tricycle (1895)

Serpollet's steam tricycle (1887)

The gyroscope has a rotating wheel (1852)

Made in 1886, the first Benz gasoline-powered car was more like a tricycle

French Panhard-Levassor. First gasoline-powered car with engine in front (1893)

A 1900 Oldsmobile from the American car manufacturer, Ransom E. Olds

A 1906 Stanley Steamer with steering wheel instead of tiller

Henry Ford's first workshop (1890-92)

The American rockaway, ancestor of the station wagon

The first Mercedes car (1901)

The first Ford car

Four-seater surrey with fringe on top (1900)

The Ford assembly-line factory as it was in 1914

Two of the Model T Fords. Fifteen million were built between 1908 and 1927

A United States mail cart (1900)

"Four wheels on the ground and one in the hands for steering. What a good idea!" thinks Peter Pebble, as he strokes his beard.

Gazing at a snappy new car from Henry Ford's factory, he wonders if he shouldn't take its five wheels for a drive. The dog has made up its mind, now it's up to Peter!

Run for it! Peter Pebble
is at the wheel!